PLACES

CONTENTS

THE FOLD-OUT PANORAMA

PeOPLE have always marveled at the great forces of nature – the wind and weather, the sun, moon, and stars – at whatever it is that keeps animals and plants growing, and the world turning.

It is not surprising that our early ancestors worshiped these forces and built vast monuments, temples, and works of art in their honor. Today, most of these early religions are long-forgotten. When we visit temples and sacred places dedicated to ancient and forgotten gods, they baffle us. It is hard to determine how these places were used – or even how they were built.

It is these mysteries that make such places so entrancing. How *did* small groups of people produce such large monuments and intricate works of art, often with simple technology? And why did they do it?

In ancient times, forces such as the weather and the stars seemed to have great power over human life. After all, if the weather was bad, the crops failed and people would starve. To these

people, there was no guarantee that the sun would rise every day. Frightening events in the sky such as an eclipse or a passing comet might mean the gods were angry.

Only the priests with their direct contact to the gods could explain the meanings of such events. This gave the priests great power, and such power allowed them to gather vast labor forces and large amounts of money to create some of the most extraordinary buildings mankind ever made. If we look closely at these mysterious places, many of the mysteries unravel. If we look closely, we can begin to understand their extraordinary power – and the power of the people who built them.

A Babylonian astronomer-priest worshiped the stars and planets as gods.

THE CAVE PAINTINGS
OF LASCAUX

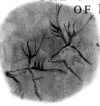

The Lascaux artists beautifully captured the antlers of these stags.

SOME of the earliest surviving art is preserved in caves in France and Spain. Among the most famous are the caves at Lascaux in France.

These caves are a system of underground chambers and passages, full of stunning paintings of people, animals (deer, horses, buffalo, cows, cats, a rhinoceros), and geometric patterns. Scientists have determined that this art was produced between 15,000 and 14,000 years ago, a warm period during the last Ice Age. The artists used pigments such as ocher (a yellow-brown clay), iron oxide (rust), and the mineral manganese dioxide (for black or dark blue). No one is sure why the

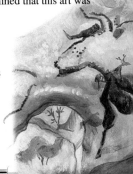

A LUCKY FIND

The Lascaux paintings were discovered accidentally in 1940 by two boys and their dog.

paintings were made, what they meant, or how the caves were used.

The caves at Lascaux are deep, and difficult to reach. It is doubtful that people lived in them. It is more likely that they were some sort of sanctuary or holy place.

Buffalo, horses, and deer are depicted in the so-called "Hall of the Bulls."

THE STANDING STONES OF CARNAC

THERE are some 3,000 standing stones at Carnac in France. They are arranged in rows that stretch for about 5 miles across the Brittany countryside. They were laid out between 4000 and 1500 B.C., and are the world's largest monument of large stones (called *megaliths*).

Carnac is in Brittany, northwestern France. Brittany was once a Celtic kingdom like ancient Britain. Druids, the Celtic priests, may have used Carnac.

Earth mounds, single stones, and stone circles discovered in the same area suggest that the region was a center for Stone-Age culture. But no one knows for sure why so much energy was spent building these monuments.

Some of the stones at Carnac are aligned so that the constellations and planets can

NAMING THE STONE

The single, solid, erect stones like those used at Carnac are called *menhirs*. This word comes from the Breton, meaning "long (*hir*) stone (*men*)."

be seen above them. The rising and setting of the moon could be observed using the alignments and a large stone called *Er Grah* or "Fairy Stone." The regular way in which the stones were laid out may have allowed people to make calculations to predict the positions of the moon and stars. Some stones are slightly out of alignment. This may be because they fell down and were repositioned.

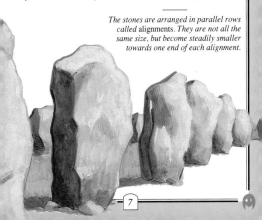

The stones are arranged in parallel rows called alignments. *They are not all the same size, but become steadily smaller towards one end of each alignment.*

THE TEMPLES OF TARXIEN

AT Tarxien on the Mediterranean island of Malta is a group of ruined buildings made of massive stones. These are among the earliest surviving temples on earth. The fine carvings on some of them suggest that they were made by highly civilized people, but the builders have long since vanished.

The temples probably date from about 3500 B.C. and were added to as time went on. Human remains have also been found here, but these were probably not the original builders.

The temples are made up of pairs of semi-circular stone rooms. The smaller rooms may have been for the priests only, while outsiders may have been admitted to the larger outer rooms.

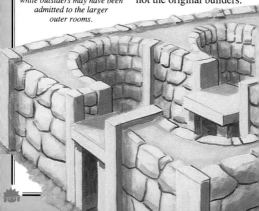

They were more likely later peoples who reused the temples as tombs.

The original of the "mother-goddess" figure found at Tarxien has lost her head, but the statue was once about 8 feet high. Her fatness could represent fertility, or a rich food supply.

Among the sculptures found on the site is a large statue of a female figure. People may have come here to worship a mother goddess, or celebrate fertility ceremonies. Some of the masonry is beautifully carved with spiral leaf patterns. This work shows the skill of the builders, who only had primitive stone tools to work with. A large *quern*, or millstone, was also found at Tarxien. This may mean that farmers brought their grain to be ground at the home of the goddess, to ensure a good harvest.

THE GREAT CIRCLE OF STONEHENGE

THIS great circle of sandstone blocks on Salisbury Plain in southern England is one of the most famous and mysterious ancient sites.

Stonehenge was built and modified over a long period between 3200 and 1250 B.C. It may have originally been a burial site. Eventually, through the addition of stones in various arrangements, it was turned into an imposing temple. The stones were aligned so that the sun rose directly above

Stonehenge was thought to contain 30 sarsen stones. These are large, grey sandstone blocks.

Some historians think that ancient Celtic priests called Druids worshiped at Stonehenge. Druids celebrated the summer and winter solstices, and considered mistletoe to be a sacred plant.

the outlying Heel Stone when viewed from the center of Stonehenge on Midsummer Day.

The huge sarsen stones that make up the outer ring were dragged from Marlborough Downs, 17 miles away, perhaps using sleds. The smaller blue-stones which stood inside the circle came from Presilis in Wales, over 300 miles away! They were probably brought to the site by glacier.

THE LOST CITY OF BABYLON

The Ishtar gate, with its glazed-brick lions, is one of Babylon's best preserved buildings.

SOME 55 miles from Baghdad, in what is now Iraq, lie the ruins of the great city of Babylon. The glittering capital of the ancient region of Babylonia once lay between the Tigris and Euphrates rivers. Babylon means "gate of god" in Babylonian.

At the ruins are the remains of nine bronze gates, and the foundations of a massive mud-brick temple – perhaps the original "Tower of Babel" mentioned in the Bible. The walls of the city were so thick that two chariots could drive side-by-side along the top of them. Many of Babylon's rulers, such as Hammurabi (1792-1750 B.C.), left written records, so we know something about the people who lived there. But we

still do not know exactly what the tower, or the famous Hanging Gardens, looked like.

Babylon first came to prominence in about 2000 B.C., when a centralized government, organized religion, and legal system were set up. The temple was first built at this time.

The Hanging Gardens were built by Nebuchadnezzar II (605-562 B.C.) for his wives. The gardens were probably roof terraces, watered by slaves who pumped up water from the Euphrates which flowed through the city.

The Babylonians had many gods and goddesses, most of whom ruled over several aspects of life. For example, Ishtar was goddess of both love and war, and Marduk, the city's patron ruler, was god of lordship, justice, the moon, and the rain.

Babylon's great temple was probably built in the form of a ziggurat, an earth mound covered with mud-bricks, with stairways outside. This sort of tower brought the priests nearer to the sky.

THE NAZCA LINES

AT Nazca near the Pacific coast of southern Peru are some of the most bewildering works of art in the world. These are lines, geometric patterns, and drawings of animals scratched on the surface of the ground.

The amazing thing about these works of art is their huge size. Most of them are too large to be seen

Scientists have recently found diagrams on pottery that show the Nazca knew how to make a hot-air balloon.

properly except from the air. The works were first discovered in the 1920s when air transport became possible. But there was no air transport as we know it when the lines were made (probably between 200 B.C. and 500 A.D., when the local Nazca culture flourished).

The drawings were made by scraping away the reddish rock that covers the ground to reveal

THE NAZCA SPIDER

The spider drawing is nearly 150 feet long and shows a reproductive organ at the end of an extended leg. Only one species is known to have this feature, which is too small to be seen by the naked eye. This species is found far away in the Amazon jungle. Perhaps the drawing is of a similar, but extinct, species.

yellow soil. The drawings have remained intact because no rain has fallen in Southern Peru to wash them away.

The Nazca people left no written records to help us understand their pictures. One scientific theory proposes that the lines make up some sort of astronomical calculator for working out the positions of stars. Another theory is that they were religious symbols. Still another theory suggests that each picture was made and cared for by a particular family, and represented some sort of ancestor spirit.

The Nazca drawings include a monkey, a snake, a whale, a spider, and 18 birds – one of which is over 900 feet long. This is the monkey (LEFT).

THE GREAT SERPENT MOUND OF OHIO

The Feathered Man, here engraved on a shell, was important in many early American cultures, including that of the Adena and Hopewell people.

S OME earthworks in North America are also shaped like animals. The most famous example is the Great Serpent Mound in Ohio, which is made in the shape of an open-mouthed snake about to swallow an egg. For the centuries since the people who made it left or died out, people have puzzled over the meaning of the shape and the identity of its makers.

The Serpent Mound (and others like it, featuring eagles, buffalo, and even human figures) was made by the people of the Adena and Hopewell cultures, which flourished between 1000 B.C. and 700 A.D. in the valleys of the Ohio and Illinois rivers. The Hopewell people were successful traders, with links stretching as far as the

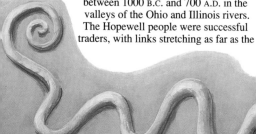

Carved soapstone pipes show another Hopewell response to the beauties of the natural world.

STAR PICTURES

One theory suggests that North American mounds were made to imitate patterns of stars. The Serpent Mound looks similar to the Little Dipper constellation.

Rocky Mountains.

The Serpent Mound is not a burial site (unlike many other mounds in the U.S.), but was clearly a religious site. Since the people left no written records, we do not know the exact nature of their religion. But the serpent is a powerful symbol in many cultures of North and South America, standing for creativity and wisdom.

An overhead view shows how well the mound was designed. In all, it is some 1,348 feet long, and winds along the top of a hill.

THE MOUNT LI TOMBS

IN 1974, workers digging wells at Mount Li in the Shensi Province of China discovered part of the burial complex of the First Emperor of China, Ch'in Shih-Huang-Ti, who died in 210 B.C. It was an enormous pit, filled with rank upon rank of lifesize clay statues of foot soldiers. These became known as the Terracotta Army. Further

Ch'in Shih-Huang-Ti built the Great Wall of China to keep out northern nomads.

The largest pit contains 3,210 foot soldiers. Some of the soldiers wear heavy armor for close combat.

pits have since been discovered, containing more soldiers, chariots, horses, and even a replica military headquarters. Thieves had plundered the pits in 206 B.C. and many weapons and metal items were stolen. But the terracotta figures remained.

Many members of the army have very little armor. They were sharpshooters who would have fired their longbows and crossbows at the enemy from a distance.

Inside the pits, each figure is an individual, obviously modeled on a real-life soldier. The detail of the statues is amazing – even the rivet heads on the armor are carefully shown. They tell us much about the Chinese army, and also about the power and importance of the man for whom they were created. But we do not know why the emperor wanted such an army about him.

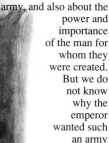

THE ROYAL TOMB OF NIMRUD DAGH

O N the border of modern Turkey and Syria was the ancient kingdom of Commagene. Between 69 and 34 B.C., it was ruled by its greatest king, Antiochus I. At Nimrud Dagh (close to Commagene's capital city,

Antiochus was buried beneath a huge conical mound of stones.

Arsameia, in what is now central Turkey), Antiochus I built his tomb. This was a great conical pyramid of crushed stones, with colossal statues and an altar for the burning of a sacrificial fire. How did the king of a small, little-known territory come to build such a place, and why did it take this form?

In Antiochus' time, his kingdom was better known than it is today. Although small, it was

Only the heads remain of many of the colossal statues. Even these are 6 feet tall.

important – it was strategically placed along east-west trade routes.

Antiochus was descended from both the Persian kings and the Macedonian leader Alexander the Great. The statues at

Statues of eagles and lions overlook the king's burial place.

Nimrud Dagh show this heritage: they often portray Greek gods in Persian clothes. The king set aside money for two monthly celebrations, commemorating his birthday and his coronation. On those days, the statues of Antiochus were crowned with gold, and incense and aromatic herbs were burned. There were sacrifices to the god-king and a feast was provided for all who came. Antiochus clearly wanted to be remembered after his death. However, in 72 A.D., Commagene became part of the Roman Empire, and the burial place was abandoned.

THE ROSE RED CITY

THE city of Petra is unlike any other. Its main buildings were carved directly out of the pinkish rocks of the Jordanian mountainsides – giving the nickname above. Why did the local people choose to create a city in this inhospitable place, and what were their buildings used for?

Between 500 B.C. and 235 A.D., when Petra flourished, two important trade routes crossed what is now Jordan. The people who lived in Petra were the Nabateans, previously a nomadic (or wandering) Arabian race who realized that they could make a living by controlling the trade that passed through the area. They guided the caravans through the rocky terrain and taxed the merchants.

Most of the surviving buildings, many decorated in the classical Greek and Roman style,

The narrow entrance to Petra is called the Siq. Beyond it lies the Khasneh.

Petra was well placed on the cross-roads of two major trade routes. One went north-south, connecting Syria with the Red Sea. The other linked the Persian Gulf in the East to the Mediterranean Sea in the West.

were first thought to be temples. It is now known that many are Nabatean tombs. The *Khasneh* is the most magnificent of Petra's tombs. People thought the urn on top of the façade was full of gold. Hopeful robbers have fired shots at it to try to obtain the treasure. We are still not really sure whether the Khasneh was a temple or a tomb. These ruins are almost all that is left of Petra, which finally fell into ruin in 1189. But 2,000 years ago the center of the city would have been bustling with shops and trader stalls.

THE MOUND CITY OF CAHOKIA

A charming pottery bottle of a nursing mother and her child that was found at Cahokia is similar in style to Mayan pottery.

NORTHWEST of St. Louis, Missouri, but on the other side of the state line in Illinois, is one of North America's most extraordinary sites. Once a city of some 40,000 people, it contains an enormous earth mound behind a plaza, more than 80 smaller mounds, the sites of thatched, plaster-walled houses, and a mass grave containing more than 300 bodies. The town's original name is lost, but it is now known as Cahokia.

The builders of Cahokia belonged to a culture that was based along the valley of the Mississippi River. The culture flourished between 800 and 1400 A.D. Strange symbols appear in the art of these people – weeping eyes, disembodied human organs, and fantastic creatures – but we do not know their meanings. They may be linked to the Southern Cult, a religion about which very little is known. Similarities between carvings from the Mississippi culture and the Mayan culture in central America suggest a possible link between the two peoples.

Monk's Mound rises 100 feet above the plaza, in five terraced levels. Its base covers an area measuring 900 feet by 600 feet. It was the site of religious ceremonies and there was once a temple on its flat top. A wooden fence enclosing Monk's Mound and 16 smaller mounds was put up at the beginning of the 13th century.

THE TEMPLES OF ANGKOR

Although built as a temple to Vishnu, Angkor Wat was later used as a Buddhist shrine, as carvings of the Buddha (ABOVE) show.

DEEP in the Cambodian jungles are the extraordinary temples of Angkor, built by the Khmer people between the 9th and 13th centuries A.D. Their canals, courtyards, and strange conical towers make them unlike any other buildings on earth. But, large as they are, they seem ill-suited for worship, and there is little trace of the people who built them.

The temples were part of the Angkor, or Angkor Thom, a great city that was once home to a million people and covered an area of four square miles.

One of the largest temples there is Angkor Wat. It was built on the orders of King Suryavarman II (1113-1150 A.D.), a renowned warrior. He intended the complex to be a shrine to his memory as well as a great temple to the god Vishnu. Khmer religion was a version of Hinduism, and the people saw their rulers as semi-divine "god-kings," so a temple was the correct dwelling place for the dead king's body. When the king died, the temple was no longer used for worship. The priests were to look after the building and pay respects to the dead monarch.

A ceremonial causeway leads to the West Gate of the temple, crossing a 625-foot-wide moat.

THE TOWNS OF CHACO CANYON

THERE are numerous Pueblo Indian settlements in the deserts of the southwestern U.S., but none are as large as the towns planned and built by the Anasazi people in Chaco Canyon, New Mexico.

The Anasazi were superb potters. Their vessels had strong geometric designs, often in black and white.

The Anasazi built 12 towns in all, but the best known is Pueblo Bonito. It is a highly planned town, semi-circular, and several stories high in some places. Why did a Stone-Age people in the middle of the desert build such a complex, well-defended structure, and what was the purpose of the strange circular rooms that form part of the plan?

The settlement was inhabited by around 1,200 people between about 1100 and 1300 A.D. The town was surrounded by strong outer walls. It once had a narrow gateway, but it was eventually blocked up. There were few windows, and the people got in and out of the town – and their houses – by using ladders. The multi-story arrangement provided for cool storage rooms at the bottom, and light living accommodation at the top. The roofs were useful working areas – cooking, pottery, basketwork, and weaving could be done here.

There were also circular rooms, called *kivas*, which were used for religious purposes. They may have had roofs, with vents for ceremonial fires.

Pueblo Bonito *is Spanish for pretty village. Spanish explorers gave the town this name in the 15th century.*

THE STATUES
OF EASTER ISLAND

ISOLATED in the Pacific Ocean, far
off the coast of Chile, Easter Island
(or Rapa Nui) has long been a
source of mystery. It is the home
of groups of colossal statues of
elongated human heads, looking
out to sea.

The statues were built
between 1100 and 1680 A.D. They
were probably carved from the
crater walls of the volcano Rana
Roraka before being taken to a site
on the coast. Here, they were put up
on temple platforms called *ahus*,
which were built by the people
who lived on the island before
the statue
builders.
When they
got a statue
to its
intended
site, the
islanders
probably
built a

*Many of the statues
have the same
features: a stylized
head and long
ear lobes. Their eyes
are painted, and some
statues have patterns
on the body that may
represent tatooing.*